PRESENTED TO

FROM

DATE

Merry Christmas and God bless you.
May you experience this season in a fresh and joyful way.

# ORNAMENTS

OF

## CHRISTMAS JOY

Meditations to Draw You Nearer
to the Miracle in the Manger

## mary grace birkhead

Design by Brand Navigation
Bill Chiaravalle, DeAnna Pierce,
Russ McIntosh & Mark Mickel

INTEGRITY
PUBLISHERS
Nashville

ORNAMENTS OF CHRISTMAS JOY

Copyright © 2006 by Mary Grace Birkhead

Published by Integrity House, a division of Integrity Media, Inc.,
660 Bakers Bridge Avenue, Suite 200, Franklin, Tennessee 37067

Unless otherwise indicated, Scripture quotations are taken from *The Holy Bible*,
New International Version (NIV), copyright © 1973, 1978, 1984, International Bible
Society. Used by permission of Zondervan Bible Publishers.

Cover and interior design: Brand Navigation, LLC. www.brandnavigation.com

ISBN 1-59145-

Printed in the United States of America
06 07 08 09 10 LBM 6 5 4 3 2 1

THIS BOOK IS DEDICATED TO MY PRECIOUS CHILDREN,

ROBERT, DANIEL, AND CAMILLE.

I PRAY CHRISTMAS WILL ALWAYS BE

A CELEBRATION FROM YOUR HEART.

I LOVE YOU.

Thank you to my husband, Rob, who keeps me focused and loves us all so much. Thank you also to: Katie Milwee, Dana Keck, Joy Patton, Anadara Arnold, Lindsay Swain, Brenda Schulte, Ellen Brandt, Sara Davis, Susan Merritt, and Courtney Connor for your sweet words of love and prayers. Thank you Sara Brewer, Dina Stevenson, and Ann Lauterback for your ornaments. Also thank you to the wonderful people at Integrity Publishers for cheering me on: Byron Williamson, Mark Gilroy, Barb James, Betty Woodmancy, Dale Wilstermann, Joey Paul, Bobby Sagmiller, and Scott Harris. And special thanks to Bill Chiaravalle and his designers Deanna Pierce, Russ McIntosh, and Mark Mickel.

# INTRODUCTION

It was usually a hot and humid December evening in Houston when my dad would take the artificial tree down from the attic. The weather outside offered no hint as to the season we were celebrating inside our house. My mom would hand the warm ornament boxes down the attic stairs, and we would listen to the Andy Williams Christmas album as we unpacked them.

I remember each year wanting a live Christmas tree and all new ornaments. Yet, as we would gingerly take out the ornaments one by one and begin to fill the tree, my desire for "new" and "different" would fade away. Some ornaments had been my mother's as a little girl. Some had been gifts to our family or bought on a special vacation. A great number of them had been made by us girls and covered in glitter and faded school pictures. I often tried to hide these handmade ones on the back of the tree so that no one would see! After all the ornaments were hung, I would wrap the tree in silver icicles to make it look like a big iced cake. Once we had completed our masterpiece, we would all go into the yard, look at our tree through the front window, and wait with anticipation for my dad to turn on the lights. Even in our shorts, T-shirts, and sandals, we knew Christmas was here!

Ornaments such as these have two special qualities, one symbolic and another decorative. They are symbolic because they reflect the season and represent a unique celebration—the birth of Christ. They are decorative because they take something ordinary such as a tree, whether it is live or artificial, and make it magnificent, pointing everyone who sees it to the miracle of the manger.

God asks us to be symbolic and decorative too. We are living symbols of the Christmas season. If we are following Him, our lives will reflect the true meaning of Christmas to others. We reflect Him in the way we love others and trust God with the details of our lives. Our attitude, our use of time, our level of anxiety, and our way of celebrating all are decorative in the fact that God is living in us and changing us! He can take our ordinary lives and make them magnificent. He can take our broken or marginal selves and heal them, restore them, refocus them, infuse them with His light, and use them to point others to the miracle in the manger.

God wants to use you. He doesn't want to hide you on the back of the tree because you don't measure up. You are created to reflect Him and to declare His praises. The moments of your life are branches upon which God can display His glory. Don't let the "weather" around you determine the attitude of the season. Christ is born! Merry Christmas!

MAKE ROOM
# FOR HIM
LUKE 2:7

*And she gave birth to her firstborn,*
*a son. She wrapped him in cloths and*
*placed him in a manger, because there*
*was no room for them in the inn.*

When your heart and mind are "full," there is no
room for Him.  Begin the day speaking His name:
"Welcome, Jesus!  Welcome into my mundane
tasks.  Come in and give me peace.  Come in and
give me joy."  He is waiting to be invited.  Swing
open your willing heart and receive Him.

WALK IN
PEACE
EPHESIANS 2:14a

*For he himself is our peace.*

Put on His cloak of peace today.
It's just your size, made just for you!
You can put on anger, bitterness, or fear,
but to wear them is to walk in unbelief.
God is more powerful than any circumstance.
Put on His robe of peace and walk in faith!

TURN TO
# THE LIGHT
JOHN 1:5

*The light shines in the darkness,*
*but the darkness has not understood.*

God can bring light to your darkness.
He longs to bring order to your chaos.
A cluttered mind has no room for God.
Choose today to turn to Him in prayer
instead of trying to manage your world.
As you take your needs to Him,
He will give you light!

KNOW YOU'RE
## NOT ALONE
MATTHEW 1:23

*"The virgin will be with child and*
*will give birth to a son, and they will*
*call him Immanuel" —which means,*
*"God with us."*

Christ needs nothing from you.  He has it all.
He desires to be with you because He loves you.
He is with you—Immanuel.  He is capable of
shouldering any care you have.  He comes along-
side to bless and care for you.  He is not tired or
worried.  He is powerful and able!  You are not
alone.  You are not abandoned.  Immanuel!

ACCEPT HIS
# FAVOR
LUKE 2:14

*Glory to God in the highest,
and on earth peace to men on whom
his favor rests.*

He wants to bless you. What lies have crept into
your thinking and keep you from believing the
truth He has for you? Are you believing you're
not good enough or you're not working hard
enough? Shake off those dead thoughts and live!
His favor rests on you!

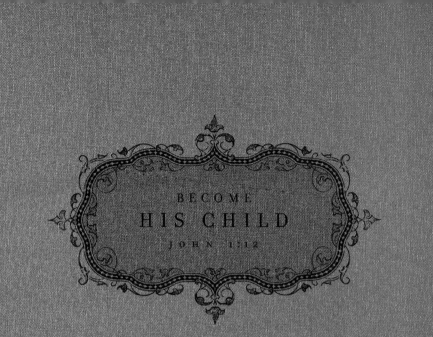

BECOME

# HIS CHILD

JOHN 1:12

*Yet to all who received him, to those who believed in his name, he gave the right to become children of God.*

God asks you to be His child—not His consultant or manager. He wants your willing, open, childlike heart. All that He asks from you is your trust and your obedience. Will you lay down your agenda and list of expectations for God and come as His child? Trust Him. He is faithful!

LISTEN TO YOUR
**SHEPHERD**
MATTHEW 2:6

*But you, Bethlehem, in the land of
Judah, are by no means least among
the rulers of Judah; for out of you will
come a ruler who will be the shepherd
of my people Israel.*

Jesus wraps Himself in humility and comes to
lead you, not to push or judge or shame you.
That is not His voice. His voice is respectful,
loving, and wise. Hear His words. Follow His way.
His voice will bring you life. Reject the voice of
condemnation and follow your good Shepherd.

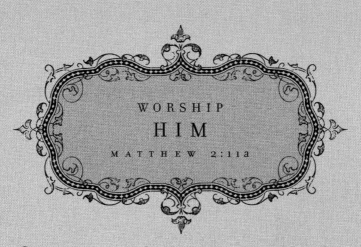

WORSHIP

HIM

MATTHEW 2:11a

*On coming to the house, they saw the*
*child with his mother Mary, and they*
*bowed down and worshiped him.*

Worship Him not because everything is
going well and every prayer is answered.
Worship Him not because you have enough
of what you need, your family is well, or because
you are at peace.  Instead, worship Him because
He is powerful and all loving.  He forgives you
for all of your sins and has a bigger plan
for your life that you cannot see.  Worship!

## FOLLOW
### THE STAR
MATTHEW 2:9

*After they had heard the king,*
*they went on their way, and the star*
*they had seen in the east went ahead*
*of them until it stopped over the*
*place where the child was.*

The star was a sign, a gift from God, to say,
Follow Me; find Me; I want to be known.
Creation calls attention to God's power and
authority. Creation testifies to the fact that
God loves unique and beautiful things.
You are His creation. Follow Him!

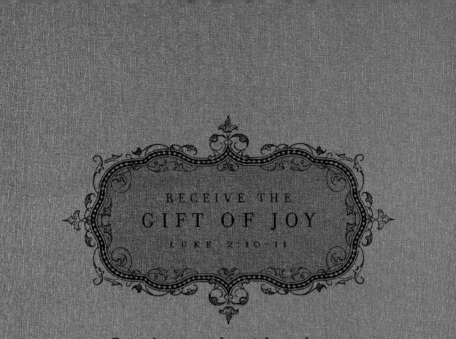

### RECEIVE THE
# GIFT OF JOY
LUKE 2:10–11

*But the angel said to them,
"Do not be afraid. I bring you
good news of great joy that will be
for all the people. Today in the town
of David a Savior has been born to you;
he is Christ the Lord."*

Christ was born for you. You are no longer
judged on your performance. He has come to
set you free! Let joy bubble out of your spirit
in celebration of that truth. Jesus dances
over you with delight—what a joy!

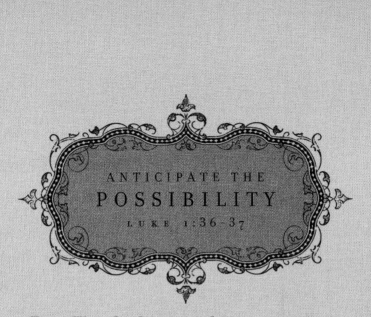

ANTICIPATE THE
POSSIBILITY

LUKE 1:36-37

*Even Elizabeth your relative is going to*
*have a child in her old age, and she who*
*was said to be barren is in her sixth month.*
*For nothing is impossible with God.*

God makes miracles happen. It is possible for
God to take this hectic day and make it amazing.
He can take the weight you carry and exchange
it for a light yoke. Are you willing? Speak your
needs to God all day—take Him with you.
Bring Him into every moment and wait for
the impossible to be made possible.

GIVE IT ALL
TO HIM
MATTHEW 2:11b

*They opened their treasures*
*and presented him with gifts of gold*
*and of incense and of myrrh.*

Pour out your cares to your Father.
Gifts, parties, travel, and children
can all be stressful blessings.
Your Father wants you to
present each one to Him.
Nothing is too insignificant;
all of your thoughts are important to God.
Let Him exchange your pressures for His peace.

GO TO GOD
## AS YOU WAIT
PSALM 130:5

*I wait for the Lord, my soul waits,*
*and in his word I put my hope.*

As you wait in line, in traffic, or on the phone,
turn your thoughts to Christ. Let Him make
the waiting time meaningful. He is right there.
Don't let your mind be distracted with worry.
Instead, let your mind be transformed by
remembering His birth! He is waiting for you!

*For to us a child is born, to us
a son is given, and the government
will be on his shoulders.*

Unto us a child is born. "Unto us" means
you and me. This is not just hope for the whole
world, but hope for you personally. Draw close
to Him. He has so much for you. He is your
Provider and Protector. He can restore what
seems broken and bring back new life.
Unto you a child is born!

PROCLAIM

# GOOD TIDINGS

ISAIAH 40:9b

*You who bring good tidings to
Jerusalem, lift up your voice with a
shout, lift it up, do not be afraid.*

Good tidings! Good news! Christ is born!
You have hope and your past is being redeemed!
Don't keep it to yourself; speak the miracle
to others! Join with the angels today in
proclaiming good tidings of great joy!

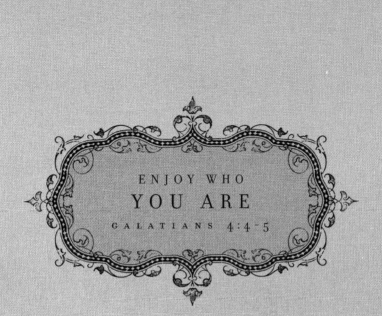

ENJOY WHO
**YOU ARE**
GALATIANS 4:4-5

*God sent his son, born of a woman,*
*born under law, to redeem those*
*under law, that we might receive*
*the full rights of sons.*

You are a child of the King! You are no longer
a slave! Like a gift certificate, your sin has
been traded for purity. As accusing thoughts
arise, practice trading them in for the truth:
You are precious, you are not forgotten,
you are loved, and you have hope!

LET
MERCY FLOW
LUKE 1:50

*His mercy extends to those who fear
him, from generation to generation.*

When you "fall short," He extends mercy.
He's not waiting to punish you. He longs to
lavish you with grace. Take the rich gift of mercy
and pour it on yourself and offer it to those
around you! He offers more than enough love,
grace, and tenderness for you to enjoy and share!

## BE HIS
# SERVANT
### LUKE 1:38

*"I am the Lord's servant,"*
*Mary answered. "May it be to me as*
*you have said." Then the angel left her.*

Be open to God's work in your life. Be flexible as
He moves in and makes changes. Be willing to
rethink and reconsider your plans; He may have
other ways of working things out. You serve the
King of the universe and He is over all things.
Are you open to being the servant of His plan?

LOOK FORWARD TO
## YOUR CROWN
2 TIMOTHY 4:8

*Now there is in store for me the crown of righteousness, which the Lord, the righteous Judge, will award to me on that day—and not only me, but also to all who have longed for his appearing.*

He has a crown waiting for you! He says you
are forgiven. He says you are His bride.
The events of this day will pass—and all the
busyness that comes with it. Let go of the
temporal. He's waiting with a crown for you.
Hold onto the promise of eternity.

CELEBRATE

# HIS GOODNESS

PSALM 145:7

*They will celebrate your abundant*
*goodness and joyfully sing of*
*your righteousness.*

He sets you free from your failures—celebrate!
He calls you His precious child—celebrate!
He longs to be gracious to you and show you
His love—celebrate! The world may be pushing
in on you, but allow your spirit to celebrate
His abundant goodness!

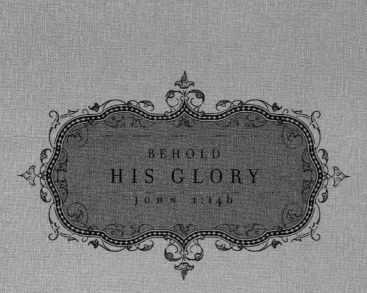

BEHOLD
HIS GLORY
JOHN 1:14b

*We have seen his glory, the glory of the One and Only, who came from the Father, full of grace and truth.*

He is the One and Only! He won't share His glory with anyone else. Don't spend your efforts seeking complete fulfillment from anyone or anything here on earth; you will only be frustrated and disappointed. Seek the Glorious One. He will satisfy your longings for approval, safety, and comfort. He is able to fulfill all of your longings.

REST IN HIS
# UNDERSTANDING
JOHN 1:14a

*The Word became flesh and*
*made his dwelling among us.*

God became flesh. He knows what it's like.
The frustrations, the pain, the disappointments,
and the inconsistencies—He knows.
You have an Advocate. One who understands.
You are not alone. He walks with you!
Celebrate God's compassion.

PRAISE HIM
FOR THE GIFT
LUKE 2:20

*The shepherds returned, glorifying and
praising God for all the things they
had had heard and seen, which were
just as they had been told.*

Do you want to be filled with same anticipation,
celebration, and adoration?  Then begin to praise
God for His gift of love:  Jesus!  Let praises
replace complaining.  Let your love for Him
be your gift to others.

STAND IN
AWE OF GOD
ECCLESIASTES 5:7

*Much dreaming and many words*
*are meaningless. Therefore stand*
*in awe of God.*

God knows your needs. Don't keep going
over everything in your mind and discussing it
with others. Give Him your list of concerns.
He does not lack the resources to
accomplish His will for you.

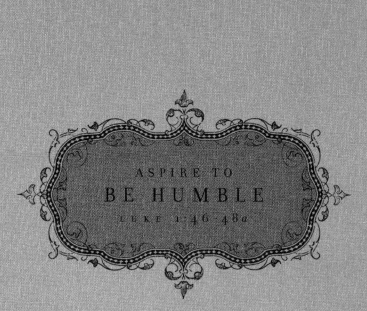

ASPIRE TO
# BE HUMBLE
LUKE 1:46–48a

And Mary said: *"My soul glorifies the Lord and my spirit rejoices in God my Savior, for he has been mindful of the humble state of his servant."*

He is watching over you. He knows your situation. He doesn't miss a thing. Let your inability to do things perfectly make you humble, not sad. Your humbleness is a canvas on which God can paint a masterpiece. Let your spirit be lifted!

PONDER
HIS PRESENCE
LUKE 2:19

*But Mary treasured up all these things
and pondered them in her heart.*

Be aware of Him this very moment.  Be aware of
His presence.  These moments are filled with
God.  Do you sense Him?  Don't miss Him in
your mad dashing about.  He is there in the chaos
and in the silence.  Ponder His place in your day.
Take His hand.  He is with you.

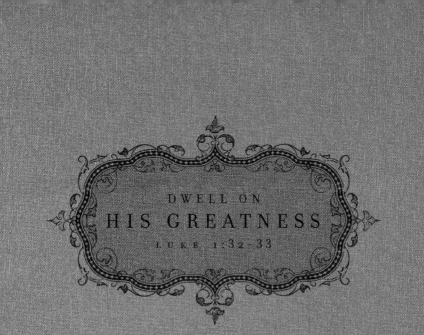

DWELL ON
HIS GREATNESS
LUKE 1:32-33

*He will be great and will be called the Son of the Most High. The Lord will give him the throne of his father David, and he will reign over the house of Jacob forever; his kingdom will never end.*

Your God reigns over all things. His power has not been thwarted, nor are His arms too short to protect you. Trust Him; don't fear this world. He is mighty to help you. Don't look at your circumstances. Look at God.

THROW OFF
**CONDEMNATION**
JOHN 3:17

*For God did not send his Son into
the world to condemn the world,
but to save the world through Him.*

You are not under the yoke of your past.
Jesus has come to set you free. You are not
under condemnation! Shame is a tool of the
Enemy who wants to steal your joy and freedom.
Throw off your cloak of doom.
He has a robe of joy for you!

WALK IN
# THE SUN
LUKE 1:78-79

*Because of the tender mercy of our God,*
*by which the rising sun will come to us*
*from heaven to shine on those living in*
*darkness and in the shadow of death,*
*to guide our feet into the path of peace.*

Your days are unpredictable, yet you can
know peace. The condition of the world is not
the condition of God! Bathe your mind in
His Word. Saturate your spirit in prayer.
Sit at rest in His presence. Peace will begin to
flow from you like a refreshing spring!